ACTIVITY LOG BOOK

Name: _____

Phone: _____

Activity Log Book

Date	Time	Name	Phone Number	Subject	Follow-up required	Initials	✓

Activity Log Book

Date	Time	Name	Phone Number	Subject	Follow-up required	Initials	✓

Activity Log Book

Date	Time	Name	Phone Number	Subject	Follow-up required	Initials	✓

Activity Log Book

Date	Time	Name	Phone Number	Subject	Follow-up required	Initials	✓

Activity Log Book

Date	Time	Name	Phone Number	Subject	Follow-up required	Initials	✓

Activity Log Book

Date	Time	Name	Phone Number	Subject	Follow-up required	Initials	✓

Activity Log Book

Date	Time	Name	Phone Number	Subject	Follow-up required	Initials	✓

Activity Log Book

Date	Time	Name	Phone Number	Subject	Follow-up required	Initials	✓

Activity Log Book

Date	Time	Name	Phone Number	Subject	Follow-up required	Initials	✓

Activity Log Book

Date	Time	Name	Phone Number	Subject	Follow-up required	Initials	✓

Activity Log Book

Date	Time	Name	Phone Number	Subject	Follow-up required	Initials	✓

Activity Log Book

Date	Time	Name	Phone Number	Subject	Follow-up required	Initials	✓

Activity Log Book

Date	Time	Name	Phone Number	Subject	Follow-up required	Initials	✓

Activity Log Book

Date	Time	Name	Phone Number	Subject	Follow-up required	Initials	✓

Activity Log Book

Date	Time	Name	Phone Number	Subject	Follow-up required	Initials	✓

Activity Log Book

Date	Time	Name	Phone Number	Subject	Follow-up required	Initials	✓

Activity Log Book

Date	Time	Name	Phone Number	Subject	Follow-up required	Initials	✓

Activity Log Book

Date	Time	Name	Phone Number	Subject	Follow-up required	Initials	✓

Activity Log Book

Date	Time	Name	Phone Number	Subject	Follow-up required	Initials	✓

Activity Log Book

Date	Time	Name	Phone Number	Subject	Follow-up required	Initials	✓

Activity Log Book

Date	Time	Name	Phone Number	Subject	Follow-up required	Initials	✓

Activity Log Book

Date	Time	Name	Phone Number	Subject	Follow-up required	Initials	✓

Activity Log Book

Date	Time	Name	Phone Number	Subject	Follow-up required	Initials	✓

Activity Log Book

Date	Time	Name	Phone Number	Subject	Follow-up required	Initials	✓

Activity Log Book

Date	Time	Name	Phone Number	Subject	Follow-up required	Initials	✓

Activity Log Book

Date	Time	Name	Phone Number	Subject	Follow-up required	Initials	✓

Activity Log Book

Date	Time	Name	Phone Number	Subject	Follow-up required	Initials	✓

Activity Log Book

Date	Time	Name	Phone Number	Subject	Follow-up required	Initials	✓

Activity Log Book

Date	Time	Name	Phone Number	Subject	Follow-up required	Initials	✓

Activity Log Book

Date	Time	Name	Phone Number	Subject	Follow-up required	Initials	✓

Activity Log Book

Date	Time	Name	Phone Number	Subject	Follow-up required	Initials	✓

Activity Log Book

Date	Time	Name	Phone Number	Subject	Follow-up required	Initials	✓

Activity Log Book

Date	Time	Name	Phone Number	Subject	Follow-up required	Initials	✓

Activity Log Book

Date	Time	Name	Phone Number	Subject	Follow-up required	Initials	✓

Activity Log Book

Date	Time	Name	Phone Number	Subject	Follow-up required	Initials	✓

Activity Log Book

Date	Time	Name	Phone Number	Subject	Follow-up required	Initials	✓

Activity Log Book

Date	Time	Name	Phone Number	Subject	Follow-up required	Initials	✓

Activity Log Book

Date	Time	Name	Phone Number	Subject	Follow-up required	Initials	✓

Activity Log Book

Date	Time	Name	Phone Number	Subject	Follow-up required	Initials	✓

Activity Log Book

Date	Time	Name	Phone Number	Subject	Follow-up required	Initials	✓

Activity Log Book

Date	Time	Name	Phone Number	Subject	Follow-up required	Initials	✓

Activity Log Book

Date	Time	Name	Phone Number	Subject	Follow-up required	Initials	✓

Activity Log Book

Date	Time	Name	Phone Number	Subject	Follow-up required	Initials	✓

Activity Log Book

Date	Time	Name	Phone Number	Subject	Follow-up required	Initials	✓

Activity Log Book

Date	Time	Name	Phone Number	Subject	Follow-up required	Initials	✓

Activity Log Book

Date	Time	Name	Phone Number	Subject	Follow-up required	Initials	✓

Activity Log Book

Date	Time	Name	Phone Number	Subject	Follow-up required	Initials	✓

Activity Log Book

Date	Time	Name	Phone Number	Subject	Follow-up required	Initials	✓

Activity Log Book

Date	Time	Name	Phone Number	Subject	Follow-up required	Initials	✓

Activity Log Book

Date	Time	Name	Phone Number	Subject	Follow-up required	Initials	✓

Activity Log Book

Date	Time	Name	Phone Number	Subject	Follow-up required	Initials	✓

Activity Log Book

Date	Time	Name	Phone Number	Subject	Follow-up required	Initials	✓

Activity Log Book

Date	Time	Name	Phone Number	Subject	Follow-up required	Initials	✓

Activity Log Book

Date	Time	Name	Phone Number	Subject	Follow-up required	Initials	✓

Activity Log Book

Date	Time	Name	Phone Number	Subject	Follow-up required	Initials	✓

Activity Log Book

Date	Time	Name	Phone Number	Subject	Follow-up required	Initials	✓

Activity Log Book

Date	Time	Name	Phone Number	Subject	Follow-up required	Initials	✓

Activity Log Book

Date	Time	Name	Phone Number	Subject	Follow-up required	Initials	✓

Activity Log Book

Date	Time	Name	Phone Number	Subject	Follow-up required	Initials	✓

Activity Log Book

Date	Time	Name	Phone Number	Subject	Follow-up required	Initials	✓

Activity Log Book

Date	Time	Name	Phone Number	Subject	Follow-up required	Initials	✓

Activity Log Book

Date	Time	Name	Phone Number	Subject	Follow-up required	Initials	✓

Activity Log Book

Date	Time	Name	Phone Number	Subject	Follow-up required	Initials	✓

Activity Log Book

Date	Time	Name	Phone Number	Subject	Follow-up required	Initials	✓

Activity Log Book

Date	Time	Name	Phone Number	Subject	Follow-up required	Initials	✓

Activity Log Book

Date	Time	Name	Phone Number	Subject	Follow-up required	Initials	✓

Activity Log Book

Date	Time	Name	Phone Number	Subject	Follow-up required	Initials	✓

Activity Log Book

Date	Time	Name	Phone Number	Subject	Follow-up required	Initials	✓

Activity Log Book

Date	Time	Name	Phone Number	Subject	Follow-up required	Initials	✓

Activity Log Book

Date	Time	Name	Phone Number	Subject	Follow-up required	Initials	✓

Activity Log Book

Date	Time	Name	Phone Number	Subject	Follow-up required	Initials	✓

Activity Log Book

Date	Time	Name	Phone Number	Subject	Follow-up required	Initials	✓

Activity Log Book

Date	Time	Name	Phone Number	Subject	Follow-up required	Initials	✓

Activity Log Book

Date	Time	Name	Phone Number	Subject	Follow-up required	Initials	✓

Activity Log Book

Date	Time	Name	Phone Number	Subject	Follow-up required	Initials	✓

Activity Log Book

Date	Time	Name	Phone Number	Subject	Follow-up required	Initials	✓

Activity Log Book

Date	Time	Name	Phone Number	Subject	Follow-up required	Initials	✓

Activity Log Book

Date	Time	Name	Phone Number	Subject	Follow-up required	Initials	✓

Activity Log Book

Date	Time	Name	Phone Number	Subject	Follow-up required	Initials	✓

Activity Log Book

Date	Time	Name	Phone Number	Subject	Follow-up required	Initials	✓

Activity Log Book

Date	Time	Name	Phone Number	Subject	Follow-up required	Initials	✓

Activity Log Book

Date	Time	Name	Phone Number	Subject	Follow-up required	Initials	✓

Activity Log Book

Date	Time	Name	Phone Number	Subject	Follow-up required	Initials	✓

Activity Log Book

Date	Time	Name	Phone Number	Subject	Follow-up required	Initials	✓

Activity Log Book

Date	Time	Name	Phone Number	Subject	Follow-up required	Initials	✓

Activity Log Book

Date	Time	Name	Phone Number	Subject	Follow-up required	Initials	✓

Activity Log Book

Date	Time	Name	Phone Number	Subject	Follow-up required	Initials	✓

Activity Log Book

Date	Time	Name	Phone Number	Subject	Follow-up required	Initials	✓

Activity Log Book

Date	Time	Name	Phone Number	Subject	Follow-up required	Initials	✓

Activity Log Book

Date	Time	Name	Phone Number	Subject	Follow-up required	Initials	✓

Activity Log Book

Date	Time	Name	Phone Number	Subject	Follow-up required	Initials	✓

Activity Log Book

Date	Time	Name	Phone Number	Subject	Follow-up required	Initials	✓

Activity Log Book

Date	Time	Name	Phone Number	Subject	Follow-up required	Initials	✓

Activity Log Book

Date	Time	Name	Phone Number	Subject	Follow-up required	Initials	✓

Activity Log Book

Date	Time	Name	Phone Number	Subject	Follow-up required	Initials	✓

Activity Log Book

Date	Time	Name	Phone Number	Subject	Follow-up required	Initials	✓

Activity Log Book

Date	Time	Name	Phone Number	Subject	Follow-up required	Initials	✓

Activity Log Book

Date	Time	Name	Phone Number	Subject	Follow-up required	Initials	✓

Activity Log Book

Date	Time	Name	Phone Number	Subject	Follow-up required	Initials	✓

Activity Log Book

Date	Time	Name	Phone Number	Subject	Follow-up required	Initials	✓

Activity Log Book

Date	Time	Name	Phone Number	Subject	Follow-up required	Initials	✓

Activity Log Book

Date	Time	Name	Phone Number	Subject	Follow-up required	Initials	✓

Activity Log Book

Date	Time	Name	Phone Number	Subject	Follow-up required	Initials	✓

Activity Log Book

Date	Time	Name	Phone Number	Subject	Follow-up required	Initials	✓

Activity Log Book

Date	Time	Name	Phone Number	Subject	Follow-up required	Initials	✓

Activity Log Book

Date	Time	Name	Phone Number	Subject	Follow-up required	Initials	✓

Activity Log Book

Date	Time	Name	Phone Number	Subject	Follow-up required	Initials	✓

Activity Log Book

Date	Time	Name	Phone Number	Subject	Follow-up required	Initials	✓

Activity Log Book

Date	Time	Name	Phone Number	Subject	Follow-up required	Initials	✓

Activity Log Book

Date	Time	Name	Phone Number	Subject	Follow-up required	Initials	✓

Activity Log Book

Date	Time	Name	Phone Number	Subject	Follow-up required	Initials	✓

Activity Log Book

Date	Time	Name	Phone Number	Subject	Follow-up required	Initials	✓

Activity Log Book

Date	Time	Name	Phone Number	Subject	Follow-up required	Initials	✓

Activity Log Book

Date	Time	Name	Phone Number	Subject	Follow-up required	Initials	✓

Activity Log Book

Date	Time	Name	Phone Number	Subject	Follow-up required	Initials	✓

Activity Log Book

Date	Time	Name	Phone Number	Subject	Follow-up required	Initials	✓

Activity Log Book

Date	Time	Name	Phone Number	Subject	Follow-up required	Initials	✓

Activity Log Book

Date	Time	Name	Phone Number	Subject	Follow-up required	Initials	✓

Activity Log Book

Date	Time	Name	Phone Number	Subject	Follow-up required	Initials	✓

www.ingramcontent.com/pod-product-compliance
Lightning Source LLC
LaVergne TN
LVHW061938070526
838199LV00060B/3861